TRUMP V GOD (HIS LAST CASE)

TRUMP V GOD (HIS LAST CASE)

BARBARA HOBART

UnBoxed Theatre Productions

www.unboxedtheatre.com

ISBN (Print): 979-8-89282-103-2

ISBN (eBook): 979-8-89282-104-9

Manuscript formatted by Kevin Theis, Fort Raphael Publishing Co., Chicago

Cover graphics by Paul Stroili, Touchstone Graphic Design, Chicago

CAST

TRUMP, 45th President
FRANKLIN, Black man, 40's
JANITOR, White man, 50's
ANNE, White girl, 13
RUDY, Black woman, 50's
IVANA, White woman, 60's
GOD, Black woman, 50's

NOTE: Dialogue that appears in quotation marks consists of actual quotes from real-life individuals.

SCENE ONE

A WAITING ROOM.

A generic space with a desk and chair at the far end of the room. Some basic office supplies include: several leather-bound ledgers in a plastic out tray, a CALCULATOR with a paper roll, a cup holder with two pencils, and a rotary telephone.

A SERVICE BELL sits next to a JAR OF LOLLIPOPS.

A LOST & FOUND box is prominent at the edge of the desk.

An OLD TRANSISTOR RADIO is at the opposite end.

A GARBAGE CAN is next to the side of the desk.

Behind the desk is an acrylic brochure holder filled with different color flyers: Red, Yellow, and Green.

There are two metal chairs on either side of a small table with old magazines: TEEN, National Geographic, and a Sears catalog. A dusty, fake ficus tree and an old doctor's office scale are in the corner.

There are three doors: The main entrance, another door marked "Private" that is situated behind the desk, and the third door is at the opposite end marked with #215.

The overhead fluorescent lights flicker and HUM.

We hear the TRANSISTOR RADIO TUNER shifting quickly between stations: STATIC NOISE, CLASSICAL CELLO, a quick DISCO BEAT, and SILENCE as...

TRUMP ENTERS and looks around suspiciously.

The flickering lights and the annoying HUM STOP.

Trump's wearing a wrinkled blue suit; his white shirt has sweat stains and a smear of mustard. His red necktie is loosened, collar unbuttoned. He looks as though he's found the right room, though not entirely sure. Holding an ice pack on his head, he takes in his surroundings.

TRUMP

Hello? Anyone in here?

He looks around, clearly agitated. He opens the door marked #215 and pokes his head in and yells into the void.

Ice machine...? I need some ice! Helllooooo? Anyone?!

Pissed, he slams the door shut. TRUMP walks to the door behind the desk marked "PRIVATE," opens it, and peeks inside.

Someone said I can find ice in here?

He waits. There is no response. The main door opens. FRANKLIN ENTERS wearing jogging pants, a T-shirt, and a sweatshirt. He's carrying a gym duffel bag. TRUMP slams the "PRIVATE" door shut.

Jesus, finally! Can you get me some ice?

TRUMP removes the ice bag from his head revealing a bruise on his forehead and hands the ice pack to FRANKLIN.

FRANKLIN
I'm sorry, do I look like I work here?

TRUMP
Yeah, well, I thought...

Paying him no mind, FRANKLIN walks to the chair drops the duffel bag on the floor and unzips it.

FRANKLIN
I know what you were thinking. I'm black, you need something, you assumed I'm here to get it for you.

TRUMP
Thanks.

FRANKLIN
I'm not. Doesn't work like that here. Thank God.

FRANKLIN sits. He removes his shoes and socks.

TRUMP
Well, do you know where I can get some?

FRANKLIN

Get in line. Everyone needs ice. It's a hot commodity. How much you willing to pay? And if you think those fancy $30 Ice Balls at Erewhon for a pack of eight is a ripoff? Wait 'til you see the price they're gettin' for plain ole cubes here.

TRUMP

I don't have any cash on me.

FRANKLIN

You? Outta cash?! Nooooo!

TRUMP

I have it... just not *on me*. Jesus, I have over five hundred million -- in cash, what do you think, I carry it around? Everyone wants my money. Like that crooked judge who thinks I'm going to pay that rigged bogus legal fee...

FRANKLIN

Judgment.

TRUMP

I'm not paying a rigged verdict. That'll happen when hell freezes over. There's a sucker born every minute and I'm not one of 'em. Seriously, do I look like I need the money?

FRANKLIN

Well, actually, yeah. You need ice. It costs money. You don't have any. So, what happened to your head?

TRUMP

Cops. Police brutality. You know.

Pissed, TRUMP tosses the ice pack onto the end table.

FRANKLIN

Well, I've been pulled over for 'Driving While Black' on numerous occasions. Fortunately, I lived to tell about it, unlike Breonna Taylor, Philando Castile, God knows how many others.

TRUMP

Who?

FRANKLIN

Philando Castile? Black man, 32, Minnesota, pulled over at a traffic stop just outside of St. Paul, shot seven times, point-blank range in front of his girlfriend and her daughter...

TRUMP

Didn't see it.

FRANKLIN

I'm guessin' it wasn't covered on that alternate-facts news channel. So, what'd they do to you?

TRUMP

Pushed me into the squad car. Hard.

FRANKLIN

Why were you in a cop car?

TRUMP

That's what I want to know! I was on my way here and was told my private driver was unavailable and they sent a cop car.

FRANKLIN laughs.

TRUMP (CONT'D)

You think that's funny?

FRANKLIN

Well, I guess they took your suggestion.

TRUMP

What suggestion?

> *FRANKLIN removes his sweatshirt, folds it neatly, and places it beside the duffel bag.*

FRANKLIN

You told 'em not to be too careful.

TRUMP

I never said that.

FRANKLIN

Yes, you did. July 28, 2017, 1:09 PM... *(imitating TRUMP from his stump speech, accordion-hands and all)* "Hey, don't be too nice to criminals... Like when you guys put somebody in the car and you're protecting their head? You know, the way you put your hand over it like don't hit their head... and they've just killed somebody?! I say, you can take the hand away, okaaaay?"

> *FRANKLIN ends with the familiar Trump smirk.*

TRUMP

You were at one of my rallies?

FRANKLIN

Look at me. If I was at one of your rallies, youd'a seen me. It was on television. Dude, everything in the universe is recorded, you can't deny shit.

TRUMP

I'm not a criminal.

FRANKLIN

That's what Nixon said. But seriously, what'd you expect? People listen to you.

TRUMP

Well, of course they do. 'Specially your people. There were many thousands -- tens of millions of black people at my rallies. I'm the most popular president.

FRANKLIN

Ex-president. And convicted felon. So, they smacked ya good. That's a hell of a boo boo on your head.

FRANKLIN laughs.

TRUMP

The most popular. I beat Abe in all the polls if you compare popularity so there is no comparison. People try to compare us, but I win. Every time. I'm the most popular by a long shot. Look, do you know where I can get some ice? I don't want a concussion and if something happens to me, it's going to be very, very bad for people. Lots of people. Heads are gonna roll, and it's not going to be mine. Get my drift?

FRANKLIN

Yeah, try the service bell. Someone should be here. They prolly on a break.

TRUMP walks over to the desk and hits the service bell. We hear a loud suction-cup sound followed by a blood-curdling scream. TRUMP jumps back. FRANKLIN howls.

TRUMP

You knew that was going to happen, didn't you?!

FRANKLIN laughs.

FRANKLIN

Oh, come on, don't get your panties in a wad. It's prolly nuthin'.

FRANKLIN removes his T-shirt, folds it, and places it beside the duffel bag. He's now bare chested.

TRUMP

Whoa. Whoa. What the hell you doing?

FRANKLIN

I have a gig in twenty minutes. My dressing room was flooded so they put me in here. I was told it would be private. What, pray tell, are you doin' in here?

TRUMP

Cops aren't supposed to arrest a President. It's unconstitutional!

FRANKLIN

Ex-president. I love it when you wrap yourself in the Constitution. Seriously, what you doin' in here?

FRANKLIN stands, takes his wallet out of his back pocket and places it on the magazine table. He takes off his pants and stands in his underwear briefs.

TRUMP

Appealing.

FRANKLIN

Why thank you!

TRUMP

Not you. I am appealing my case! Put your pants back on. What the hell do you think you're doing?!

FRANKLIN

Relax. You're not my type.

FRANKLIN sits and reaches into his duffel bag and removes a pair of black fishnet hose. He smiles and winks at TRUMP.

Aw, come on, lighten up. I'm not hittin' on you. Just having some fun, that's all.

FRANKLIN puts on the fishnet stockings.

TRUMP

Who the hell are you?!

FRANKLIN

Franklin D. Merriwether, but my Drag Queen name is Eileen Dover. What's yours?

TRUMP

What...? I don't have a drag queen name... what the hell is going on here?

FRANKLIN

Oh stop, everyone has one. And a Porn Star name!

He breaks into "STORMY WEATHER" for a couple of bars.

Didn't you play the Porn-Star-Name-Game when you had sleepovers?

TRUMP

I didn't have sleepovers...

FRANKLIN

Well, that's the problem! You didn't have any fun growin' up with that Nazi father of yours. Come on, let's get you one. What month were you born?

TRUMP

I'm not playing this game --

FRANKLIN

Oh, hush. Don't be a sourpuss... what month were you born?

TRUMP remains silent. FRANKLIN stands and adjusts the fishnet hose.

(sing-song) I can Google it...

TRUMP

June.

FRANKLIN

Ok, so June babies are always a "Dame."

TRUMP

A what?

FRANKLIN

A Dame! Depending on the month, you could be a Madame, a Miss, a Lady... Queens need a title, everyone knows that!

TRUMP

Excuse me?

FRANKLIN

It's simple, it works like this: the first letter in your first and last name corresponds to a month and a title. The only reason I remember June is for *Dame* is because my ex was born in June. Fucker. Okay, so, the first initial of your first name is "D" for Donald -- or Donna as we like to call you behind your back... and hey, don't blame me -- Randy Rainbow started it. Anyway, "D" stands for...

FRANKLIN removes a cheat-sheet from his duffel bag, looks it over, and HOWLS with laughter.

Gurrrl... I couldn't make this up if I tried! *(perusing the rest of the sheet)* Okay, the first letter of your last name is T... which is always in HUGE letters on everything... Do you know how many hundreds of thousands of selfies are posted of people giving the finger while posing in front of Trump Tower? There's an entire Facebook group...

TRUMP

I told you I was popular. Especially your people.

FRANKLIN

So, you said! But back to you... I probably underestimated -- I bet there are MILLIONS of posts giving you the finger, forgive me, I've never been good with numbers, but then again, neither are you! We're practically soul sisters! So, where was I? T... "T" corresponds to... OH MY GOD, what are the odds? This is just too perfect... Are you ready?! Sit -- sit!

TRUMP remains standing.

Fine, be a spoilsport. Your Drag Queen name is... Drumroll: Dame Hedda DeClass -- LOVE it!

FRANKLIN gives three wildly flamboyant three finger snaps in the air. TRUMP is not amused.

Well, if you don't believe me, see for yourself.

With a grand gesture, he hands TRUMP the cheat sheet.

I'll wait. Or just choose one -- you don't HAVE to go by this, though it is the quintessential Drag Queen Name-Game Cheat-Sheet.

TRUMP

I don't want a Drag Queen name! I want some ice!

Pissed, TRUMP walks over to the empty chair, sits, and tosses the cheat sheet onto the end table -- which covers FRANK'S wallet. TRUMP then picks up The National Geographic and TEEN Magazine. He opts for TEEN and opens it.

FRANKLIN

Fine. Be that way.

FRANKLIN returns to his seat, turns his back on TRUMP as if he were a scorned lover. FRANKLIN reaches into the duffel bag and removes a padded bra that he puts on and adjusts. TRUMP peers over the magazine and looks on, somewhere between shock and intrigue.

TRUMP

I definitely need ice. I'm seeing things.

FRANKLIN

Damn straight. These titties aren't for everyone!

FRANKLIN removes a black velvet tank top from the duffel and puts it on. Next, he removes a silver-sequined skirt that he steps into and zips up from the side. With a "keep a distance" (talk to the hand) arm gesture, FRANKLIN saunters over to the door marked #215, opens it, and looks at himself in the mirror on the inside of the door. He contemplates his outfit...

I don't know.

TRUMP

Looks good. Except, there's a loose thread hanging in the back...

FRANKLIN tries to see where it is but can't. He shimmies over to TRUMP for help.

FRANKLIN

Can you pull it? And please, don't let me unravel! God knows I don't want to embarrass myself at the event!

TRUMP puts down the magazine. He finds the thread, tries to sever it but can't. He leans in, bites it off, and hands it to FRANKLIN.

FRANKLIN (CONT'D)

Well done. Thanks! Looks like you've had some practice, big guy.

FRANKLIN playfully pokes him on the shoulder.

TRUMP

At my inauguration, Melania had a loose thread. Not to mention loose lips.

FRANKLIN

No. With who? Do tell!

FRANKLIN sits down and leans in close to TRUMP.

TRUMP

Everyone. The Press, Putin, Pence. That's just the "P's."

FRANKLIN

Women! Can't trust a thing that comes out of their mouths. Amiright?

TRUMP

Her mouth is as loose as her pussy.

FRANKLIN taken aback, yet doesn't miss a beat...

FRANKLIN

Mm hmm. All liars. Every gat damn one of 'em.

TRUMP

They manipulate and twist every word.

FRANKLIN

Sister, I know you know! And not to mention, ungrateful!

TRUMP, clueless he's being played --

TRUMP

Tell me about it.

FRANKLIN

After all you did for her? Gurl... she owes you.

TRUMP

Big time. Did you know, I got her fast-tracked for citizenship, brought her whole damn family over, and that's the thanks I get?

FRANKLIN

Outrageous. You ask me? You should have 'em deported. All of 'em.

TRUMP

I like the way you think.

FRANKLIN

And I thought you only liked me for my girlish figure!

FRANKLIN playfully slaps TRUMP with the back of his hand. TRUMP lightens and laughs for the first time.

Immigrants. They're all the same. They come here looking for a free ride and everything's handed to them on a silver platter. Not like you, no siree, Bob.

TRUMP

I worked hard for every penny.

FRANKLIN

(breaking into DONNA SUMMER) HARD FOR THE MONEY! Right?! It's not like your daddy wrote a check for you!

TRUMP

You're right, I should have them all deported.

FRANKLIN

Damn straight. You need to show them who's Hedda DeClass! See? It's fate, that's the perfect drag name for you. You own it. But wait a sec, what about Barron?

TRUMP

What about him?

FRANKLIN

When you deport Melania... I mean, he's just a kid, he needs his mother.

TRUMP

He needs to man up. No son of mine is going to be a pussy.

FRANKLIN

How do you explain Eric? Kidding -- KIDDING! Sorry, just playin' -- I'm sure Barron will be fine.

TRUMP

He's a good kid. He just needs to toughen up. No one respects a pussy.

FRANKLIN

'Specially you!

TRUMP

So, what exactly are you getting ready for here?

FRANKLIN

Third Friday of every month we have a gala. It's sort of an over-the-top graduation party if you will. I'm headlining -- sold out. You're coming, right?

TRUMP

Uh, no. I don't have a ticket.

FRANKLIN

No worries. I'll pull some strings and get you on the wait list... Hedda DeClass to Hedda DeLine!

FRANKLIN gives another three finger snaps.

It's going to be filled to the rafters. Granted, I'm not nearly as popular as you, but I do have a following. Check my Instagram. If you follow me, I'll follow you back. *(feigning modesty)* You know, I'm a celebrity, too.

FRANKLIN removes a wig cap from his duffel bag and puts it on. Next, he removes a blonde wig, bends over, places it on his head, then whips his head back and shakes out his golden locks.

And we know what special privileges we get as celebrities.

Franklin is now in full drag. Uncomfortable, TRUMP stands, reaches for the ice pack, and starts to make his way to the main door.

TRUMP

Well, it's been great talking to you. I need to be going...

FRANKLIN grabs him by the shoulder and spins him around.

FRANKLIN

(threatening tone) Where do you think you're going?

                              TRUMP
I need to find some ice...

                            FRANKLIN
I didn't give you permission to leave.

> *FRANKLIN runs his finger down the front of TRUMP'S shirt. After a beat, FRANKLIN shoves TRUMP, pushing him hard against the wall. FRANKLIN strokes TRUMP'S cheek. TRUMP drops the ice pack.*

                              TRUMP
Get your hands off of me. Stop...!

> *FRANKLIN grabs TRUMP'S cheeks and kisses him hard on the mouth.*

                            FRANKLIN
What'd you say on that Access Hollywood tape? "I don't even wait. And when you're a star, they let you do it. You can do anything - grab 'em by the pussy. You can do anything."

                              TRUMP
I never said that...

> *FRANKLIN stares at TRUMP and wipes his mouth.*

                            FRANKLIN
Yeah, you did. How 'bout grab ` em by the balls? Like this --

> *FRANKLIN grabs TRUMPS' crotch. In pain, TRUMP squirms.*

TRUMP

Stop! It was out of context. The fake news was out to get me... I said STOP! -- Let go of me!

TRUMP tries to get out of his grip but can't.

FRANKLIN

Did you stop when those women asked you to? When you forced yourself on them?

FRANKLIN tightens his grip. TRUMP yelps in pain.

TRUMP

Let go of me! I didn't force myself. I don't have to. They wanted it.

FRANKLIN

Wanted it? How many?

TRUMP

All of them! They're all lying bitches!

FRANKLIN

Bitches? So, you're the victim?

TRUMP

Hell yeah. They're coming out of the woodwork to get money and fame. That's what they want.

FRANKLIN

So, E. Jean was lying when she said you assaulted her in the dressing room?

TRUMP

Damn right. I never met that ugly bitch in my life. She's not even my type! She and her dyke attorney are the ones who are gonna pay. They made it all up. There's not a shred of evidence! There were no cameras back then so it's her word against mine!

O.S. STAGE MANAGER'S VOICE

This is your half hour call. Half hour to places.

FRANKLIN loosens his grip and steps back. TRUMP remains against the wall, frozen.

FRANKLIN

Get on your knees.

TRUMP

What?

FRANKLIN

Kneel. On your knees.

FRANKLIN raises his hand above TRUMP'S head in a fist. Slowly, in complete fear, TRUMP cowers and kneels.

FRANKLIN

Bow.

TRUMP

What...

FRANKLIN lowers his hand until it touches the top of TRUMP'S head. TRUMP bows his head... which FRANKLIN pats.

FRANKLIN

Bow wow. Good little bitch.

FRANKLIN walks over to his duffel bag, removes a black feather boa and swirls it around his neck. He puts the rest of his clothes inside the duffel bag and picks it up... LEAVING HIS SHOES.

FRANKLIN

There's evidence. The universe records everything. Every action. Every thought.

FRANKLIN walks toward the main door.

Every. Single. Deed.

Franklin EXITS. The fluorescent lights above flicker and the annoying HUM resumes.

SCENE TWO

TRUMP remains on his knees. Shaken, he looks up at the ceiling and all around to see if he's being watched.

After a beat, he picks up the ice pack and slowly stands. He tries to steady himself and mutters --

TRUMP

Person. Woman. Man. Camera. TV. Person. Woman. Man. Fucker. Faggot.

TRUMP wipes the back of his hand across his lips leaving Franklin's lipstick smeared on his sleeve. TRUMP straightens his shirt and jacket.

A JANITOR ENTERS carrying a toolbox. He's wearing a one-piece coverall and work boots.

TRUMP

Hey, you see that guy who just left?

JANITOR

Uh, no, sir... sorry. What'd he look like?

TRUMP

A woman.

JANITOR

Didn't see anyone. Is something wrong?

TRUMP

I want him arrested. I want him locked up.

JANITOR

Why? What happened? What he do?

TRUMP

He... kis... never mind, I'll get my people to deal with him.

JANITOR

You okay? Can I get you anything?

TRUMP

I'm FINE!

JANITOR

Okay, sure. Whatever you say. I'm just going to fix...

The JANITOR walks to the door marked #215.

TRUMP

Okay... yeah -- ice. I need some fucking ice.

JANITOR

I'd like to help, but I'm sorry, we're all out. *(off Trump's shaken demeanor)* Look, I'm supposed to be fixing the smoke detector... The last interview got a bit heated shall we say and blew the fuse -- but hey, let me see what I can find for you. I'll do my best.

TRUMP

Thanks, man. You do that, I'll remember you.

TRUMP gives him a thumbs up and a fist pump. The JANITOR nods and EXITS.

TRUMP picks up the ice pack and tosses it onto the end table and notices FRANKLIN'S WALLET.

He picks it up and looks inside. He removes several large bills. He looks at the LOST AND FOUND BOX. He opts to put the bills into his jacket pocket.

He places FRANKLIN'S empty wallet into his back pants pocket.

After a beat, he sits and notices the TEEN MAGAZINE which he picks up and scans with interest.

We hear the TRANSISTOR RADIO TUNER shifting quickly between stations: STATIC NOISE, CLASSICAL VIOLIN, a FEW BARS FROM "Every Night About This Time" (1942) by The Ink Spots, and --

ANNE ENTERS. She's wearing a simple, grey linen dress, white shirt, white ankle socks, and a pair of worn, brown leather shoes. She's holding a tin can.

The fluorescent lights stop flickering, the annoying HUM STOPS.

TRUMP looks up from the magazine.

TRUMP
(flirtatious) Well, hello, young lady.

He tosses the TEEN magazine on the end table and flashes a smile.

ANNE
Hello.

TRUMP
Are you lost, too?

ANNE

No. I'm collecting donations.

TRUMP

For what?

ANNE

To help kids in need.

TRUMP

What do they need?

ANNE

Many things... food, medicine, shelter, clean air and water, we need to make sure they have a safe tomorrow.

TRUMP

I've donated millions to charities. Especially to kids' charities. Hundreds of millions.

ANNE

That's very generous. Would you like to make a contribution?

She extends the tin can. TRUMP removes Franks's wallet, opens it, and shows her it's empty.

TRUMP

I'd love to but I don't have any cash on me.

ANNE

Thank you, anyway. Have a good day.

She turns to leave.

TRUMP

Wait... uh... do you happen to know where I can get some ice? Some loser janitor said he'd get some but I don't have any faith in him and I really need to refill this --

He picks up the ice pack.

ANNE

We have very little water, it's a precious resource. We need to conserve. I'm sorry but I can't give it to you.

TRUMP

There's plenty of water. What are you talking about? It's everywhere.

ANNE

Ice is really expensive for many reasons, for one, the earth is changing...

TRUMP

No, it's not.

ANNE

It is. It's heating up, the Polar Caps are melting...

TRUMP

Oh Christ, don't tell me you bought into those bullshit liberal talking points.

ANNE

Antarctica is melting at a rate of about 150 billion tons a year, Greenland -- almost 270 billion tons every year adding to the sea level rise.

TRUMP

See? The sea is *rising*! There's lots *more* water! And if that's the case, it's great because that "means basically you have a little more beach front property."

ANNE

No, it's the exact opposite... the ice sheets store about two-thirds of all the fresh water on earth and we are *losing* ice...

TRUMP

Global warming is a hoax. "Ice storm rolls from Texas to Tennessee. I'm in Los Angeles and it's freezing. Global warming is a total and very expensive, hoax!"

ANNE

It isn't. Scientists have proven it's true.

TRUMP

That's what the liberal media wants you to believe, but it's a lie. A big lie. Fake news. Junk science. Believe me, I know more than they do. "In the 1920's, people talked about global cooling. They thought the earth was cooling! Now, it's global warming! And actually, we've had times where the weather wasn't working out, so they changed it to extreme weather." They have all different names. It's to confuse you.

ANNE

What if you're wrong? What if you're destroying tomorrow for your kids and your grandchildren?

TRUMP

I'm never wrong.

ANNE

Everyone is wrong sometimes.

TRUMP

Not me. Look, you want proof? Here's proof -- look at winter: The "brutal and extended cold blast could shatter ALL RECORDS - whatever happened to Global Warming?" Huh?! Nope. I'm not a believer in that science mumbo jumbo. I believe there's weather." Those fake scientists are wrong. When you get older, you'll see I'm right. That's what I tell my granddaughter, Arabella. You remind me of her. What's your name?

ANNE

Anne.

TRUMP

I think you two are about the same age. How old are you?

ANNE

Thirteen.

TRUMP

I thought so. See? Told you, I'm never wrong. Arabella is the same age. She just had a Bat Mitzvah. You know what that is?

ANNE

I do.

TRUMP

My daughter, Ivanka, converted for her Jew husband. They threw Arabella a huge party. Ivanka loves pretty things, she loves getting dressed up, throwing big parties, spends money just like her mother, you know.

ANNE

I never had a big party. Or a Bat Mitzvah.

TRUMP

Are you Jewish?

ANNE

I am.

TRUMP

Too bad. Well, to tell you the truth, Arabella isn't a real Jew.

ANNE

What do you mean?

TRUMP

They say it is passed from the mother, through blood you know, so converting doesn't really count. They're fake Jews -- in name only. So, what'd you get for your big birthday?

ANNE

Kitty.

TRUMP

A cat? That's a very special gift. Be careful though. Immigrants eat pets.

ANNE

Kitty is my diary. I picked it out myself. My parents surprised me.

TRUMP

That was very nice of them. Why did you name it Kitty?

ANNE

I need someone to talk to.

TRUMP

You don't have any friends? *(flirtatious)* A pretty girl like you?

ANNE

No. Not anymore. They all went away.

TRUMP

Maybe you'll get some new ones. I have many friends. I'll be your friend. It's good to have friends, but only if they're loyal. If they're not, get rid of 'em. Fuck 'em. So, besides Kitty, what else did you get?

ANNE

Oh, that was more than enough. I like to write. I want to be a writer.

TRUMP

I mean, what do you like to do for fun? Go out? Go to the movies, with your boyfriend, maybe?

ANNE

I'm not allowed to go out.

TRUMP

Pretty girls should have boyfriends. Do you have a boyfriend?

ANNE

No. Maybe someday, I hope. For now, I just focus on my writing and look out the window when I can. It's where I get to escape and dream.

TRUMP

Windows are good. I like windows. "They want to take a building, and they want to make the windows from nice windows to little windows. I mean, they literally want to take buildings down and rebuild them with tiny little windows, okay? Little windows so you can't see out, you can't see the light." What do you like to look at?

ANNE

"I take a long, deep look at God and nature. Not at the houses and rooftops, but the sky. As long as you can look fearlessly at the sky, you know you will find happiness once more."

TRUMP

I've looked fearlessly at the sky, too. Looked right at the sun during the eclipse. Everyone told me I needed those special glasses, but that's not true, I didn't.

ANNE

What happened?

TRUMP

Nothing! I proved all of them wrong -- as usual. Looked right at the sun. That's the secret of my success: do whatever the hell you want. Defy everyone.

ANNE

What about God?

TRUMP

He's okay.

TRUMP gives a big 'thumbs up.'

ANNE

I meant, do you believe in God?

TRUMP

Me?! Hell yeah, I'm the biggest believer! No one is a bigger fan than I am... In God We Trust!

TRUMP does a fist pump.

So, what do you like to write?

ANNE

Everything. My dreams. "Sometimes I can't say what I think so I write it down because no one understands me. It helps to put down my fears as well as my hopes. It's a desperate time to speak the truth."

TRUMP

Tell me about it! I'm the most outspoken, the most misunderstood, and the most silenced. No one has ever been more silenced than me! They try to shut me up with gag orders but it doesn't work... and that's when you double-down. Turn the screws tighter and keep speaking your truth. Don't be afraid and never let anyone take away your voice. They'll try but they can't.

ANNE

I wish I could, but it's impossible to speak freely. Everyone is afraid, especially my parents. I know they feel helpless, which is the worst kind of fear, not being able to protect their children, yet we all try to act hopeful

ANNE (CONT'D)

and pray for another day. I hope to one day become a journalist so people will know the truth.

TRUMP

You don't want to be one of them.

ANNE

Why not?

TRUMP

Because "I know words. I have the best words." Trust me, journalists twist everything. They're scum bags.

ANNE

Why do you say that?

TRUMP

They lie. They're the lowest scum of the earth. And no offense, but the media is run by Jews. They control everything. They are the true enemies of the people.

ANNE

Are those the best words you can find?

TRUMP

It's just a figure of speech.

ANNE

Jews are not the enemies. My parents, our relatives and friends... me... we are not the ones in control.

TRUMP

Okay, not everyone in the media is bad. There are a few good ones who speak the truth. Hannity, my good buddy, Tucker, Alex Jones, all great Americans.

ANNE

Are they Jewish?

TRUMP

No.

ANNE

So, when you say: "Jews control everything," that's not the truth. What you're saying doesn't make sense. Why would we turn against ourselves with lies about ourselves that make us the most hated people on earth?

TRUMP

Hey, don't take everything so literally. You're too young to be so cynical. No one hates you.

ANNE

They do hate us. "Antisemitism has cropped up in circles where once it would have been unthinkable." *Literally.* People we thought were our friends turned their backs. It all began with words from the media, from you... words that demonize Jews have turned into hateful deeds.

TRUMP

Hey, not everyone hates the Jews. I love Jews. No one loves them more than I do!

ANNE

Even the fake ones?

TRUMP

Look... it'll be fine. This is adult stuff. You shouldn't worry your pretty little head. You're young, you have your whole life ahead of you.

ANNE

I would like to think so but I don't know what the future or tomorrow holds for myself or the world. I hope I will live a long life. But I wonder how much longer we can survive like this. "It's difficult to dream of the future when faced with this grim reality."

TRUMP

You need to lighten up. Like I said, you're too young to be so negative.

ANNE

I agree. No child should have to live like this. No one of any age should.

TRUMP

Here's the truth: There are good and bad times where people like us are misunderstood.

ANNE

People like us?

TRUMP

Yeah. I've been in tough situations no one thought I would ever get out of -- not in a million years, and look -- I'm still here! Stronger and more powerful than ever. You'll have great stories to tell when you grow up.

ANNE

I do not believe we are alike. And I don't know if I will ever understand what we did to make people hate us so. "If I do live to become a journalist, I will set the record straight so it will never happen to anyone else."

TRUMP

There are always two sides. People believe what they want to believe. And I can make them believe anything.

ANNE

Like what?

TRUMP

Making them feel like they're on top, that they're in control. That's all people want: to feel powerful -- and that's what I give them.

ANNE

How?

TRUMP

Easy. People see themselves as victims.

ANNE

Some people *are* victims. They've been brutally attacked and victimized. Even killed.

TRUMP

Well then, it's their fault.

ANNE

How is it their fault?

TRUMP

They didn't pick the right side. Look, people are tired of scraping and clawing their way to the middle. When they finally get there, they're afraid they'll lose what they have and because people are greedy -- they always want more.

ANNE

Some people might be greedy. Not all.

TRUMP

Nope. It's human nature. Want to know the secret? People are stupid. Especially my followers. Give someone a nibble and soon they'll be eating out of your hand. When people *think* you believe in them, it gives them hope and that's when they start to rethink what they've always believed in and then they begin to question themselves.

ANNE

You're saying hope breeds doubt?

TRUMP

One hundred percent. And that's the beauty. It's easy to get people to rethink their beliefs. And that's when you have your *in* and that's when you double down. Once people get a taste of power, they'll do anything to hold on to it and they'll fight like hell to keep it. Then, when given a choice, people choose a side -- the winning side, my side, because everyone wants to win.

TRUMP gives another fist pump.

ANNE

I wish we could fight back. I wish I could stand up to them. "But they come for us in the night, go house to house. I see them from my window when it's dark... long lines of innocent people with crying children ordered about by a handful of men who bully and beat them until they drop. No one is spared. Parents and children are ripped apart... the sick, the elderly, children, babies, and pregnant women at the mercy of the cruelest monsters to ever stalk the earth. And all because they're Jews. It's a wonder I haven't abandoned all my ideals, they seem so absurd and impractical. Yet I cling to them because I still believe."

TRUMP

In what?

ANNE

"That in spite of everything, people are truly good at heart."

TRUMP

That's true. There are good people, "very fine people on both sides."

ANNE

No. There are no "very fine" Nazis.

She turns to leave.

I will be a writer. I hope my words will survive even if I do not. Good luck to you.

TRUMP

Yeah, thanks. Get out there and live it up, kid.

She EXITS. The lights flicker and the annoying HUM begins.

Then, a BLACKOUT.

In darkness, WE HEAR a steel door shut followed by a lock.

The LIGHTS FLICKER ON and the HUM resumes.

TRUMP looks down where Anne stood and notices her pair of brown shoes.

SCENE 3

We hear the TRANSISTOR RADIO TUNER shifting quickly between stations: STATIC NOISE, A TRUMPET, a FEW BARS FROM "Who's Sorry Now?" (1923) Isham Jones.

The fluorescent lights stop flickering as --

RUDY G. ENTERS carrying a large, very heavy black trash bag.

RUDY

There you are! I've been looking everywhere for you. Where the hell have you been?!

TRUMP

Here. Waiting for some stupid janitor to bring me some ice. Can you get some? I'm tired of waiting.

TRUMP picks up the ice pack.

RUDY

Hell no. I'm done being your go-fer. But, if I did it would cost you. Big time.

TRUMP

Done? Who the hell are you?

RUDY

What do you mean, 'who am I?' You know damn well who I am. You owe me!

TRUMP

I don't owe you anything. I don't even know who you are.

RUDY

$148 million ring a bell?

TRUMP

What?

RUDY

Rudy.

TRUMP

(Searching for a name) Rudy... ???

RUDY

Giuliani. Rudy Giuliani. What, you hit your head so hard you don't know who I am?

   Silence.

TRUMP

You don't look like the Rudy I know.

RUDY

What?

TRUMP

Firstly, I didn't hit my head. I am the victim of police brutality. And they are gonna pay ME -- big time. And as far as I know, Rudy Giuliani isn't black.

RUDY

Excuse me?! I'm sick of your bullshit games. When it came time for a pardon, after all I did for you? Nada. I busted my ass for you and your lies. Claiming you don't recognize me ain't gonna fly.

TRUMP goes to the door marked #215, opens it, and reveals the full length mirror on the inside. RUDY stares at himself.

TRUMP

I don't owe you anything.

RUDY

What the fuck? Is this some sort of a trick mirror? This isn't who I am -- wait a second, here, I'll prove it: look at my license...

RUDY takes out his wallet from his pants pocket, removes his drivers license, and hands it to TRUMP, who reads it.

TRUMP

Ruby Freeman.

RUDY grabs it back and looks at it. He continues to stare at himself in the mirror.

RUDY

I was wondering why people were calling me racist names.

TRUMP

Well, we do live in America.

RUDY

Ruby? This is insane. That's not who I am. I don't know any Ruby except for -- wait a minute...

TRUMP

Except for who?

RUDY

That woman we accused in the election in Georgia.

TRUMP

We?

RUDY

Yes, WE! The election worker and her daughter, Ruby Freeman and Shaye Moss.

TRUMP

I didn't accuse them. You did.

RUDY

I did it for you... on your behalf!

TRUMP

Well, that's not what the court found. They found you to be liable. $148 million, you said?

RUDY

PLUS, all of the legal fees you stiffed me on not to mention what you owe me for my blood, sweat, and tears.

TRUMP

Yeah, I remember your sweat. Pitiful. Hair dye dripping down your cheeks. So, how do you explain your new "look?"

RUDY

I can't. Except this feels a lot like the bullshit alternate universe you've created and I can't get out. I'm stuck.

TRUMP

How long you been like this?

RUDY

I don't know. After the trial, someone shouted: one day you will know what it feels like to walk in her shoes.

TRUMP

Who said that?

RUDY

No idea. It was a voice I heard. It felt distant at first but at the same time it felt like it was right inside my head. Loud. Penetrating. It resonated to my core... then, right after the trial...everywhere I went store owners would follow me around as I entered their shops. I got pulled over when driving for no reason... then, no matter where I went, people shouted death threats at me and said I tried to rig the election!

Rudy stares at himself in the mirror.

To TRUMP:

You see who I am, right? You know, it's me, Rudy, right?

TRUMP

I see you for who you are; you embarrassed me.

RUDY

I embarrassed you? When?!

TRUMP

Too many times to count. The Four Seasons press conference... but the hair-dye incident was the kicker.

RUDY

I was out there peddling your truth. Or should I say, your lies.

TRUMP

Lies?

RUDY

The ones about Ruby and her daughter tampering with the ballots. I'm getting accused of rigging the election we tried to pin on them!

TRUMP

Well, you said you'd get the evidence. No one twisted your arm.

RUDY

There was no evidence!

TRUMP

And whose fault is that? You said you'd get it and you didn't.

RUDY

Because it doesn't EXIST! There is no evidence!

TRUMP

You believe that?

RUDY

It's not just me! Everyone told you it was a clean election and you lost...Meadows, Bill Barr, Pence, everyone at Homeland Security, the God damn Justice department... Ivanka and Jared started packing for Miami for fuck sake!

TRUMP

You believe I lost?

RUDY

I've always believed in you, but you lost. Everyone knows that except you!

TRUMP

Not true. The people who matter the most believe it and THAT'S WHAT COUNTS. My followers believe I won and that's what matters!

RUDY

But we can't prove it!

TRUMP

YOU can't prove it. That was YOUR job. Your one fucking job and you blew it! Thankfully, my followers believe me and they're willing to do anything. They've proven it. Now, if you want to go sit on the losing side, so be it. But don't come crawling back to me to save you from yourself. You said you would prove I won and you didn't. So, who is the real loser here?

RUDY

You!

TRUMP

Excuse me? Did you just call me a loser?

RUDY takes a step backwards.

RUDY

Yes, I mean... no, I was saying... I was loyal to you. More loyal than any-one! I didn't flip on you like Jenna, or Michael, or Hope Hicks...

TRUMP

Hope hurt. That one I didn't expect. Shame. She has a great ass.

RUDY

... I was saying I lost everything... my house, my reputation, my job... I filed for bankruptcy, I'm getting death threats -- and through it all, I stayed true to you! None of them did. I did! I stayed loyal!

TRUMP

Thanks.

RUDY

"Thanks?" That's all you got, "thanks?!"

TRUMP

Look, Rudy, we go back a long way. You were always one of my favorites, but what can I say? Things change. People change. You changed. Not me... I didn't change. That's what makes me who I am. I am as transparent as they get. You chose to believe in me. You wanted your day in the spotlight again, to be recognized -- to be seen. I gave that to you. Tenfold. Right?

RUDY

You did.

TRUMP

I did that because I thought you were a true friend.

RUDY

I am. The truest. We go back decades. We had some fun times over the years.

TRUMP

We did. But now you come to me begging for help to get you out of your mess? I'm tired of cleaning up people's messes. Your mess! Get the hell out of my sight!

TRUMP flicks the back of his hand, shooing him away.

RUDY

What?

TRUMP

You heard me. You're a pathetic loser... who the hell do you think you are coming here to accuse me of owing you?! Huh? You created your fate!

Rudy steps back in fear. SILENCE. They stare at one another.

RUDY

You're right. I was out of line asking you for help.

TRUMP

And?!

RUDY

And I'm sorry. Really. I didn't mean to bother you with my troubles. Hey, there's no other co-conspirator I'd rather be tied to!

RUDY laughs, trying to make light. TRUMP is silent.

Not funny. Okay, look, why don't we put all of this behind us and re-claim your destiny. You won. We just -- *I* just need to prove it.

TRUMP

That's what I like to hear. Now, give me some time to think about your apology.

RUDY

Of course. Take as much time as you need. Shall I wait outside, boss?

TRUMP

No, you go take a walk. And while you're at it, get me some ice. I'm tired of waiting on that stupid janitor. You think you can handle that?

TRUMP dangles the ice pack.

RUDY

Of course. Yes, Donald. Not a problem. I'll be right back.

TRUMP

And a Diet Coke.

RUDY

I'm on it, boss. Thank you. Thank you.

RUDY bows his head in deference and EXITS.

The fluorescent lights flicker. The annoying hum resumes.

TRUMP notices RUDY'S SHOES.

SCENE 4

TRUMP tosses the ice pack on the end table.

TRUMP

Loser.

TRUMP sits and picks up the TEEN Magazine once again.

We hear the TRANSISTOR RADIO TUNER shifting quickly between stations: STATIC NOISE, A PIANO, a FEW BARS FROM "Love is a Many Splendored Thing" (1955) Four Aces.

After a beat, IVANA ENTERS. The fluorescent lights stop flickering, the annoying HUM STOPS.

She is dressed in a black pantsuit, white shirt, and black pumps. The only pop of color is her bright red lipstick. She is wearing black sunglasses - full wrap that covers the side of her eyes.

TRUMP is startled.

IVANA

A goat shit on my plot.

TRUMP

What?

IVANA

You heard me: a fucking goat shit on my plot! Really Donald, you bury me on your golf course and don't have the decency to take care of it? The weeds are overgrown and I am not going to be pissed on any more. I had enough of that with you.

TRUMP

What's going on here? You have a nice spot -- right by the first hole...

IVANA

Burying the mother of your children on your golf course for tax credits is low -- even by your standards. Only you would think of designating a golf course for cemetery use.

TRUMP

You have a prime location. What are you complaining about? You're right next to the first tee!

IVANA

So, that means wifey number two will be buried on the second hole and Malaria will be planted on the third?

TRUMP

Melania.

IVANA

Whatever. You have no shame. Never did. I am sick of being humiliated by you. It never ends. But it will now.

TRUMP

Hold on here -- I thought you were...

IVANA

Dead? Only in your heart. Isn't that what you told me when we split? Well, apparently, you got your wish. Now it is so. You should know, however, the cause of my death seems suspicious to many.

TRUMP

Look, I don't know what kind of joke is being played on me...

IVANA

On you? How the hell is it that you are always the victim?! How is this about YOU?!

TRUMP

I put you on the best spot. You want me to dig you up and put you where? Next to the snack shop?! Would that be more dignified? And from the look of things, it looks like you've been eating there regularly.

IVANA

You should talk! How many cheeseburgers have you choked down? How 'bout your mug shot in Georgia? You put down your weight as 215? HA! More like how many pounds you've gained. *(She points to the door marked #215)*

TRUMP

I weigh 215 pounds.

IVANA

Where? On Mars? Your weight is going up like the number of your convictions. You can't lie to me, Donald. I have your number. All of them.

TRUMP stares at her.

TRUMP

Christ, I'll have my people get the weed-whacker and clean up your space. We good now? Hey, do you know where I can get some ice? I can't count on Rudy. He's a moron.

IVANA

You're just figuring that out now? He's a fucking idiot. And no. We aren't "good" now. Everyone who has ever been within an inch of their life isn't "good." You've fucked everyone who has come into your orbit. What amazes me is everyone thinks they will be the exception. If you want ice, call room service!

IVANA goes to the desk and is about to ring the service bell.

TRUMP

No! Don't ring that...

IVANA rings the Service Bell. We hear a suction-cup sound followed by a blood-curdling scream. She laughs.

I don't know what kind of joke you're pulling here, but if this is about money, you were well compensated after the divorce.

IVANA

For my silence. For keeping your secrets. That is my biggest regret. No more.

TRUMP

Excuse me -- we have an NDA.

IVANA

Had. Til death do us part. And I'm glad to be free of you. I can no longer sit by silently. I need to speak the truth. Whatever the cost.

TRUMP

What the hell does that mean?

IVANA

I can't live like this anymore!

TRUMP

You're dead!

IVANA

Life does not stop at death.

TRUMP

What?

IVANA

You claim to be so smart, figure it out! I'm finally done playing your losing game. I need to move on. I stood by as you did what you... *do*. I pretended not to see. I watched you look at our daughter in a way no father should.

TRUMP

You were always jealous.

IVANA

I wasn't jealous, I was disgusted by the way you spoke about her with your friends and allowed them to speak of her as a piece of meat. Remember when Howard Stern said she was "a good piece of ass?" I do. And I made sure when you brought your friend Jeffrey Epstein around,

IVANA (CONT'D)

she was nowhere to be seen after you took her and Eric to lunch with him. That was the last time. She was twelve! Parents are supposed to protect their children. What do you have to say for yourself?

TRUMP

Nothing happened.

IVANA

She was exposed to that monster... something no little girl should have had happen. You don't have an "I'm sorry?"

TRUMP

For what? She's fine.

IVANA

How would you know that? You've never had a real conversation with her. Donald, is there anything, one thing, *something* you can apologize for?

TRUMP

Not that I can think of.

IVANA

One thing. Donald... think of *one* thing. It will save you!

TRUMP

From what?

IVANA

Yourself.

TRUMP

Wait, don't tell me... you've found religion, too? No thanks. I'll take my chances.

IVANA

Don't. You are all out of chances. I'm not going to remind you of all the things I know. What you know I know.

TRUMP

You can't prove anything.

IVANA

I can't, no. But time does not erase history or facts. Time is a place holder. Time holds the secrets. *Everyone's* secrets. Your secrets. Every last one of them.

TRUMP

Are you threatening me?

IVANA

It's not about threats. It's about owning up to what has happened and facing one's own destiny. My destiny. I finally chose mine. Yours will come sooner than you think. I needed to move on... no matter what the cost. I looked back and wondered how I looked the other way, not just with Ivanka... but with the boys. They deserved a real father, not that you would have taken them fishing or played ball with them like most other fathers, but you taught them to be greedy and mean and to hunt. To kill animals for trophies and get trophy wives, which is why Eric and Don Jr. turned out as they did -- like you: assholes. Don't turn a blind eye to the truth like I did, Donald. There is no escaping it.

She removes her sunglasses revealing she has one eye, the other is just a black hole where the other once was. TRUMP looks away, disgusted.

TRUMP

Put those back on. I can't look at... that.

IVANA

Of course you can't. Because you're a weak, sad, little man. A bully wrapped in a lie. I see you now for what you are. But more importantly, I finally see myself for who I am. I'm as guilty as you are for how they were raised and I hope one day I may be forgiven throughout time, though I doubt I will ever be able to forgive myself.

She puts the sunglasses on and EXITS. The fluorescent lights above flicker and the annoying HUM resumes.

A spotlight rises on Ivana's shoes.

SCENE 5

TRUMP paces. He walks around trying to clear his head.

TRUMP

Person. Woman. Man. Camera. TV. Person. Woman. Man. Mother. Fucker. Woman. Bitch.

Pissed, he sits down and picks up the TEEN Magazine. He flips through several pages and then hurls it across the room. He looks at his watch. He leans back in the chair, folds his arms, and taps his foot on the floor.

The fluorescent lights stop flickering as --

GOD ENTERS. She is wearing a pair of black pants, a floral top, and a work apron. She's carrying a toilet plunger in one hand and a large, leather-bound ledger in the other.

GOD

Mercy on me! I would have been here sooner, but there was a flood on the second floor... nothing epic like that Noah situation, but I tell you, it caused a whole lotta problems!

She places the ledger on the desk.

GOD (CONT'D)

Frank's dressing room needs new carpet but fortunately, we caught it before it leaked down to the Pickleball courts -- I tell you, if I don't take care of things, they don't get done.

She opens the door marked "PRIVATE" and places the plunger inside. Next, she removes her apron, places it on the inside hook, and shuts the door. She sits at the desk, clasps her hands, and gives TRUMP her full attention.

So, what do you need?

TRUMP

Ice.

She slaps the top of the table.

GOD

That you do! Ask and you shall receive!

She stands, opens the door behind her desk marked "PRIVATE," and steps inside.

We hear an ice machine dispensing ice. She emerges with a 16 oz cup of ice.

GOD

Let there be ice! Here you go.

Stunned, TRUMP approaches her. She hands him the cup.

TRUMP

Thanks.

She returns to her desk and sits. While leaning back in her chair, she observes the following:

TRUMP takes the ice pack from the end table and opens the lid. He fumbles as he pours the ice cubes into the pack and several spill out onto the floor. He doesn't bother to pick them up. He tightens the lid and places the ice pack on his forehead. He remains standing.

GOD

I'm all ears. How can I help you?

TRUMP

I'm here to speak with the person in charge.

GOD

You have my full attention.

TRUMP

I mean the person who runs things.

GOD

That would be me.

TRUMP is reluctant, but continues.

TRUMP

I received this notice from The Society of Universal Theorists. Who do I speak to? I'm here for my hearing -- I'm appealing my case.

TRUMP reaches inside his jacket pocket and removes an envelope, which he hands to her. GOD opens it and peruses the letter.

GOD

Denied.

TRUMP

I know that! It says right there I was denied admission. No one denies me. That's why I am appealing. I haven't had my official hearing!

GOD removes a rubber stamp and an ink blotter from the desk drawer. She stamps the letter, places it back into its envelope, and returns it to TRUMP.

GOD

It's official now.

TRUMP

Excuse me? When did I have this hearing?

GOD

When you entered this room. It has just concluded.

TRUMP

Look lady, who the hell is in charge here? I don't have time for this shit.

GOD

I'm in charge. And that is true, you don't have a lot of time left. You failed the test.

TRUMP

I didn't fail at anything! I never fail. What test?

GOD

You've been given tens of thousands of chances to move ahead.

TRUMP

When?

GOD

During your lifetime, you were presented with opportunities to do the right thing to redeem yourself.

TRUMP

I haven't done anything!

GOD

True. I really wanted you to succeed, make the right choices, do better, be better, yet you still couldn't find an ounce of empathy for anyone.

TRUMP

Name three. First two don't count.

GOD

Well, for example... you could have put Frank's wallet inside this Lost and Found bin. Instead, you pocketed the money. Then, when you had a chance to pay it forward -- not even with your own money -- and contribute to help Anne's charity, you lied and said you didn't have any. With Rudy, all you had to do was acknowledge your part, but you let him take the complete fall. With Ivana -- simply apologize. We're done here. You are being released. And that's four things. All count.

TRUMP

Released? To where?

GOD

To complete your life section on 'Earth Two' and then you will be placed under supervision.

TRUMP

Earth Two?

GOD

We needed a name for what was happening over there. When you tried to create an alternate universe with "alternative facts" the name practically coined itself!

GOD laughs.

TRUMP

Okay, I get it, this is a huge joke like Candid Camera. Ha. Ha. I bet Roger Stone set this whole thing up. He's quite a joker! I get it.

TRUMP shouts toward the ceiling:

Roger, you got me! Good one! Where's Bannon? He in on this?

GOD

Mr. Stone had nothing to do with this, he's currently facing his own challenges. Same for your friend, Steve. It appears he is starring in his very own real-life sequel: *Orange Is The New Orange.*

TRUMP

Wait! What do you mean "placed under supervision?"

GOD

When the universe is... how shall I put this, "off kilter," it corrects itself. It needs to step in, so to speak.

TRUMP

It?

GOD

The universe... *it* is a vast machine. Been like that since the beginning of time -- which, I may add is still by far the greatest mystery... its age is still unsolved after billions of years. I love that challenge!

TRUMP

Challenge?

GOD

The universe sets out challenges. People solve them. You heard about the two high school girls Calcea Johnson and Ne'Kiya Jackson who solved the two-thousand-year-old Pythagorean theorem?

TRUMP

Uh, no.

GOD

Two young black girls from St. Mary's Academy came up with an in-genious geometric construction and together, with the law of sines and a convergent infinite sequence, proved the theorem! Probably wasn't covered on Fox.

TRUMP

Thrilling. What does this have to do with me?

GOD

Ah, yes, of course. You. As one who likes to be the center of the universe, your role in it has been reevaluated. You're being set back. Sort of like having to repeat second grade.

TRUMP

I didn't have to repeat second grade!

GOD

No, you didn't. I believe your father paid for your advancement. But that's not why we're here. It was just an example of the way things work in the universe. Let's walk this back and begin at the beginning. Well, not that far back but -- *your* beginning and why you received that notice. Please, take a seat. Would you like a lolli?

> *GOD removes a lollipop from the jar on her desk and offers it to him.*

> *TRUMP defiantly remains standing. He folds his arms across his chest and smirks.*

> *After a moment, the lights flicker and go black.*

> *There is darkness for five seconds: We hear a dramatic thunderbolt.*

> *Two seconds later, we hear a kazoo. The lights come up, no flicker. TRUMP is sitting in a chair opposite her desk. He is sucking on a lollipop. GOD blows the kazoo one more time.*

GOD

I love this thing! Cracks me up, every time. You want to know more?

TRUMP

No.

GOD

The first kazoo was made back in the 1840's by a German American clock maker named Thaddeus von Clegg who was credited with the invention.

GOD (CONT'D)

But the truth is it was an African American folk music instrument invented by a man named Alabama Vest, a former slave... To this day, Thaddeus is still working for Mr. Vest.

TRUMP

Thanks for the history lesson, lady, but all that slavery stuff could have been avoided.

GOD

Really? How so?

TRUMP

Negotiation. I could have negotiated The Civil War. "That war was so horrible. Lincoln could have avoided so much bloodshed, so many mistakes were made. So many people died. You know, that was the disaster. That war... it was a tough one for our country. Abraham Lincoln, of course, if he negotiated it, you probably wouldn't even know who Abraham Lincoln was." Except for the assassination attempt. I survived mine. Abe didn't. Loser.

GOD

That's an interesting take on history.

She puts the kazoo in the desk drawer.

As I was saying, the universe operates under a set of rules, laws, and facts... THEORIES. These are not untested hunches or guesses without supporting evidence. Things that "might be" or "could be possible" don't fly. In *reality*, a theory is a well-substantiated, proven explanation of an aspect of the world that incorporates laws, hypotheses, and facts. It is science.

GOD stands, opens the door marked "PRIVATE," and removes a 2nd-grade level diagram:

For example, the theory of gravity explains why apples fall from trees and why astronauts float around in space. The theory of evolution explains why people exist on earth. When new ideas are introduced that grab hold of people's imaginations -- without evidence, they set things off course and an alternate reality tries to take over, there needs to be a correction.

TRUMP

Aren't new ideas -- good?!

GOD

Not when they aren't new. Or good. Like global warming becoming a new real estate opportunity for investing in beach front property. Throughout history, people have stolen ideas, case in point: the kazoo. Others have repeated ideas and tried to make them *seem* new... While many ideologies took hold over periods of time, they were ultimately defeated...That's when 'do overs' take place to advance to the next stage.

TRUMP

I'm not doing anything over. I have no regrets.

GOD

It's not about your regrets. It's about ours.

TRUMP

Ours?

GOD

The Society.

TRUMP

Society loves me!

GOD

The Society of Universal Theorists.

TRUMP

Who the fuck are they?

GOD

A collective of individuals who have contributed significantly to the development of society and ultimately the universe.

GOD opens the desk drawer and removes a bag of lollipops and re-fills the jar.

TRUMP

No one has made more contributions than I have. I've made many thousands of contributions to society!

GOD

That is not up to you to decide. That judgment is left to others. And time.

TRUMP

How the hell does that work?

GOD opens her desk drawer and removes a BAG OF POPCORN and hands to TRUMP.

GOD

A panel reviews and monitors events and actions during specific periods -- life sections if you will, and their findings are then presented.

TRUMP

And who is on this "panel?" Wait, don't tell me, a bunch of liberal Democrats?

He munches on the popcorn.

GOD

It's too long a list, but suffice it to say, from the beginning of time, a lot of great thinkers, artists, painters, inventors, leaders, scientists, and others decide who is recommended to move forward for the greater good. From there, those selected enter a new phase -- or realm where they can expand their work and after all is said and done, we have a big potluck. Last week, DaVinci came up with a brilliant twist on an Arrabbiata sauce!

TRUMP

And the rest who don't move forward?

GOD

They do it until they get it right.

TRUMP

What the hell does that mean?

GOD

Some people cannot decide where they stand, so we make that possible for them.

TRUMP

How?

GOD

By walking a new path.

TRUMP

Uh huh. And how long, pray tell, is that?

GOD

Depends. Everyone has a different journey. Time is not measured by hours or seconds or years... but rather, by what they have learned. Some never move on.

TRUMP

Like who?

GOD

Well, there have been trillions of people over the course of time and virtually everyone goes back a few times to move forward. Then, there are those in the "Millionaires Club," the top one-percenters.

TRUMP

I've always been in the top one percent.

GOD

That's true. You are in an elite group.

TRUMP

So, who exactly is this information presented to that decides?

GOD smiles. She then holds up the rubber stamp.

GOD

That would be me.

TRUMP

You. You are the "decider?"

GOD

Yes.

TRUMP

HA! I thought that was Dubya! Didn't he like to call himself "The Decider?!"

TRUMP continues eating the popcorn.

GOD

That he did! On several occasions! It was funny until, well, it wasn't.

TRUMP

So, Dubya's "moving on?" Guess anyone can pass!

GOD

While I cannot comment on individual cases, he needs some more "education," if you will. Sort of like your friend, Rudy. You see, the universe meets people where they are at. Sometimes it's after they pass on -- as in the case of your ex-wife, Ivana. Other times it's during their lifetime, like Rudy. And then there are people who move through time and the universe like Anne Frank and share their wisdom and knowledge.

TRUMP

I see. And where pray tell is Rudy "at."

GOD

At the moment, looking for ice. We've met him at his "later-in-life" challenge. We've met him at several junctures during his lifetime.

GOD (CONT'D)

This round he's in the midst of facing several choices he needs to make in order to move ahead. As I mentioned earlier, he's walking a new path, this time in Ruby's shoes... where he is experiencing firsthand what it feels like to be on the receiving end of his own actions.

TRUMP

How's he doing?

GOD

Not as well as I had hoped. It doesn't look promising but I've been surprised before.

TRUMP

Don't hold your breath. That moron couldn't find ice in an igloo. Okay, let me get this straight... YOU are the ultimate "decider?!"

GOD

In the flesh. Well, in a way you can understand.

TRUMP

I don't understand. I thought you'd be...

GOD

Taller? *(God laughs.)* I know you don't understand and I get it. We've never actually spoken before. I've never, not once, heard you call out my name -- not even in a foxhole prayer. Even Ron Reagan Jr. blurted out my name -- twice! Granted, he had a little help the second time when he stubbed his toe on the coffee table... the expletive which followed was excused, but he did utter it!

TRUMP crumples up the bag of popcorn.

TRUMP

Reagan, Junior? He's a poof.

The JANITOR ENTERS carrying his toolbox and a small cup of ice.

JANITOR

Oh, excuse me. I didn't mean to interrupt. I can come back.

GOD

No worries, Max. Come on in.

JANITOR

I was just going to fix the smoke detector and I found this cup of ice for Mr. Trump.

The JANITOR approaches them.

GOD

Where did you find it?

JANITOR

I didn't. It's from my own reserve. I figured he needed it more than I did.

GOD

That's very kind of you.

TRUMP

Thanks, buddy. I knew you'd come through.

Trump reaches for the cup of ice.

GOD

That won't be necessary. I gave Mr. Trump what he needs. You keep it. Go back to work, don't mind us!

JANITOR

Thanks, boss.

The JANITOR nods and walks to the other side of the room and places his toolbox on the floor. He opens the door marked #215 and removes a step ladder. He climbs the ladder and removes the old smoke detector from the ceiling and begins to assemble the new one. He listens to their conversation as he works.

TRUMP

So, "boss," you're claiming to be God, prove it.

GOD

I don't have to prove my existence. It's your job to prove you are worthy of yours. But I'm pretty sure you will get the proof you want in no time.

TRUMP

Sorry, lady, but I'm not buying any of this.

GOD

No need to apologize. Though, it would have helped if you were able to do so with your ex.

TRUMP

Yeah. That'll happen when hell freezes over!

GOD

I love that people still believe hell exists! And heaven. Oh, the expressions people come up with: *"There's gonna be hell to pay!"*

GOD (CONT'D)

I've noticed you like using catastrophic threats to scare people like "if I'm indicted" or "if I'm convicted, hell is going to rain down death and destruction the likes this country has never seen." I'm impressed. That's a "hell" of a rainstorm you can produce.

TRUMP

My followers can.

GOD

Death and destruction?

TRUMP

They're very powerful.

GOD

Apparently. Six people died on January 6th.

TRUMP

I never killed anyone.

GOD

Your followers did.

TRUMP

They're grown men and women. No one made them.

GOD

Well, you did prod them on, no?

TRUMP

They're passionate. What can I say? They don't want to be lied to. They're defending me.

The JANITOR removes the old smoke detector and continues working.

GOD

Even though it's a lie you created?

TRUMP

They don't know that.

The JANITOR continues to listen as he works.

GOD

Wonder what your passionate supporters will do when they find out the truth and who lied to them?

TRUMP laughs. The JANITOR stops working for a moment and listens closely.

TRUMP

Go ahead, try it. Many people tried to get them to believe otherwise. Good luck with that! They believe in me. Nothing and no one can change that. They're willing to die for me. I can't help it if that's how they want to show their loyalty.

GOD

It shows me they're deluded. Killing in your name is no justification.

TRUMP

Well, I guess we're even: sometimes they kill in yours.

He shoots the crumpled bag of popcorn toward the garbage can. He misses.

GOD

That doesn't make us even.

TRUMP

Does in my book. So, if there is no heaven or hell, what is there?

GOD

What you make it. What you create. It's all in your hands. Not mine.

TRUMP

You just said you are the decider! And by the way, I don't know why people keep talking about my hands. They're not tiny.

GOD

Life is a series of challenges. What you do with them and where you end up is your choice.

TRUMP

Oh, please. That sounds like one of those feminist, vegan, lesbian, de-mocrat, immigrant-loving, bleeding-heart-liberal bumper stickers they put on the back of a Prius! No thanks.

GOD

I believe you left out a few groups to add to that list of those you dis-dain... which is odd because as I recall, your grandfather and two of your wives were immigrants. Any more questions before you're on your way?

TRUMP

No. You've wasted enough of my time. And for the record, my hands are not tiny.

She opens the desk drawer and removes a brown paper bag. With each food item she mentions, she reaches into the drawer and places each into the bag.

GOD

Here's a little snack for your journey. You like string cheese, right? I mean, who doesn't? An apple from my garden, and a cookie from the Baking With Biker Chicks Bake Off. I snagged the last one! It's gluten free.

She places the cookie into the brown bag, folds the bag nicely, and hands it to TRUMP. He stands, grabs the snack bag, and slams it into the garbage can.

TRUMP

LISTEN, LADY, WHOEVER THE HELL YOU SAY YOU ARE, YOU DON'T KNOW WHO YOU'RE TALKING TO! I DON'T THINK YOU KNOW WHO I AM!

Silence.

GOD

I do. I don't think you know who you are. That's the problem.

TRUMP

I know God damn well who I am! Now, I need to get back to Mar-a-Lago.

GOD

You will not be going back there. But you will be joining other one-percenters.

TRUMP

That's a given. Where am I going?

GOD

As a member of the Millionaires Club, you will be traveling to a number of places.

TRUMP

Is that so? How long? I have a busy schedule.

> *GOD removes the RED FLYER from the wall of brochures and hands it to TRUMP. She then opens the leather-bound ledger and looks inside.*

GOD

We'll arrange transportation.

TRUMP

I only fly private.

GOD

Uh huh. I have your itinerary, no worries. Those who are a part of this elite group have killed or harmed a minimum of one million people. So, you'll be traveling for quite some time.

> *She removes a pencil from the cup and turns on the calculator.*

TRUMP

I haven't killed or harmed anyone! Are you insane?!

> *TRUMP goes to the main entrance and tries to open the door. It is locked.*

GOD uses the eraser tip of the pencil as she punches the numbers into the calculator...

GOD

From here on, you will retrace the footsteps of every single person you have harmed and the lives they've touched. Just like your friend Rudy is doing. Think of him as an example of your future. You will re-live each of the days from beginning to end to understand what they endured.

TRUMP

You're out of your fucking mind!

GOD

During Covid, four hundred thousand people died while you were in office. Instead of trying to find a solution and save lives, you tried to suppress evidence of the existence of the virus because you didn't want the number of deaths to make you look bad. Then, you told people to drink bleach as a cure. Seriously? Bleach? That's the best you could come up with?

He stops struggling with the door.

TRUMP

I came up with many things. Hydroxychloroquine, light therapy...

GOD

Yes, we remember that idea: "hitting the body with tremendous, very powerful light inside the body." I'm not sure I recall a time the panel was rendered completely speechless. Let's just say, *light* is my department. Stay away from that one. Next time, best you keep your "bright" ideas to yourself, or better yet, consult with an actual doctor or scientist. Each of the four hundred thousand souls who died left behind loved ones. When you add in fathers, mothers, daughters, sons, children,

GOD (CONT'D)

grandparents, who all grieved their losses, we're looking at upwards of 1.2 million who were harmed.

TRUMP

Those numbers are rigged! And more people died under "Sleepy Joe..."

GOD

The term "rigged" is getting really tired. Get another word or a thesaurus. Let's get this straight: the universe doesn't "rig" anything. It has an accurate count of every event, thought, action, and deed since the beginning of time. If you would like to review our accounting ledger and all of the supporting evidence -- *including tapes* -- it will be provided to you along with your exit papers. You with me?

TRUMP

I'm not going anywhere. You can't make me.

GOD

Want to double down on that? Let's play a game: I'll be the rainmaker.

She reaches for the Service Bell. Before she taps it, TRUMP sits.

Good. Here are the ground rules: stop with the name calling. It's juvenile. You sound like a two-year-old. "Sleepy Joe," "Lyin' Ted," "Crooked Hilary," it's pathetic. And regarding your Hilary obsession, don't even think about bringing up "her emails," they don't work here.

TRUMP

She deleted thirty-three thous... *(God raises her right hand wide open. She closes her fingers to her thumb indicating for him to stop talking which he does mid-sentence.)*

GOD

STOP! Now understand this: the life sentence you are about to receive is about *you* and what *you* are responsible for. At this very moment you are at the center of the universe. MY universe.

TRUMP

Listen, I have an idea, let's talk about this, I've been thinking...

GOD

Don't. Thinking has never ended well for you. You'll just make it worse for yourself *(under her breath)* if that's possible.

> *GOD punches in numbers; the calculator paper roll begins to unwind.*

Let's begin with the people who worked for you and stiffed. The Taj Mahal, your casino. I believe you referred to it as "The eighth wonder of the world." Impressive. That's right up there with creating light. Hundreds of small contractors, carpenters, electricians, plumbers, worked on building "the eighth wonder" lost their businesses, homes, and filed bankruptcy because you didn't pay them.

TRUMP

"You have to be very rough and very tough with most contractors or they'll take the shirt right off your back..."

> *Once again, she raises her hand to put him on "Mute."*

GOD

The only clothing removed was what you stripped them of. You walked away owing them several hundred million dollars. These people employed tens of thousands of workers who also couldn't be paid, and you left them all shit out of luck.

GOD (CONT'D)

But, as everyone knows, shit rolls downhill. At this juncture, you are at the bottom of that hill, knee deep. Without boots.

GOD punches in more numbers. The paper roll gets a bit longer.

TRUMP

Let's discuss this... maybe I didn't get their invoices. Maybe Allen didn't pay them -- I have many people who handle payroll...

GOD

No, you don't. It's all you. You decide where every penny goes, every invoice that gets paid, every decision about who gets stiffed and who doesn't. Mr. Weisselberg who is currently doing time on Rikers Island for you -- why is beyond me -- didn't stiff them. You did.

GOD punches in several more numbers. She continues reviewing the ledger.

Moving on... over six thousand migrant families and two thousand six hundred and fifty-four children you put into cages were separated from one another. Four of the adults died by suicide. Allegations of sexual assault and rape of the women and children while in custody have been documented.

TRUMP

When you come to this country illegally, you pay the consequences.

GOD

Revenge on the innocent isn't a "consequence." It's cruelty.

TRUMP

My followers disagree. They elected me to clean up the country.

GOD punches more numbers into the calculator.

GOD

Well, to coin one of your favorite phrases: "you're fired."

TRUMP

From what?!

GOD

The head of "housekeeping." As for your followers... this brings us to some of your favorite people: White Supremacists and Nazis. Those you chose to call "very fine people" who marched through the streets with Tiki Torches holding signs proclaiming "Six Million Wasn't Enough" and "Jews Will Not Replace Us." Do you condemn their rhetoric?

TRUMP

The beauty of this country is the freedom to speak freely.

GOD

It's odd you find beauty in such hateful speech. Do you condemn it?

TRUMP

Everyone deserves to be heard.

GOD

I will take that as a "no." Next: what about women?

TRUMP

What about them?

GOD

Do they have the freedom to say what happens to their bodies?

A long pause.

TRUMP

You think you're clever, don't you? Trying to "get me." I've always been clear on this issue. Very clear. It's not up to me.

GOD

In 1999, you gave an interview...

GOD turns on the TRANSISTOR RADIO. We hear the MEET THE PRESS intro and then:

TRUMP'S VOICE (OVER RADIO)

"I'm very pro-choice. I hate the concept of abortion. I hate it. I hate everything it stands for. I cringe when I listen to people debating the subject. But you still – I just believe in choice."

TRUMP

That was before I was elected. I have every right to change my mind.

GOD

So, you now have rights over women?

TRUMP

It's not up to me.

GOD

Who is it up to?

TRUMP

The people! "Now the states are deciding. It's taken it off the shoulders of the federal government. Always they wanted it to be decided by the states. And Roe v. Wade didn't do that. So now states are voting on it. And in many cases, it's more liberal. In many cases, not in all cases. In some cases, they're going the other direction. But the people are deciding. And in many ways, it's a beautiful thing to watch."

GOD

More "beauty." I see. So, the "people are deciding?" Aren't women... *people?* Shouldn't they be deciding for themselves? Men don't have laws governing their bodies, why should women?

TRUMP

What is this, a witch hunt?

GOD

Hardly. I'm just asking you to state your opinion on a woman's right to choose what she can do with her own body.

TRUMP

Whatever she wants. There, I said it. Are you happy?

GOD

Are you going to tell that to your followers and supporters?

TRUMP

I just told you. It's out of my hands. The Supreme Court decided.

GOD

Exactly. The court decided... not women. And your hands played a huge role in making sure the court took away a woman's choice.

TRUMP

MY HANDS ARE NOT TINY!

GOD

Let's discuss another group of people for whom you showed no compassion. People like Serge Kovaleski.

TRUMP

Who?

GOD

Serge Kovaleski. The reporter with muscular dystrophy you imitated in front of crowds mocking his disability. Flailing your arms -- which he is unable, jerking your head wildly, quivering and contorting your hands and body and stuttering as you tried to humiliate him. It's interesting you are so sensitive about your hands when you have no compunction mocking his. I find this shameful and astonishing.

> *TRUMP looks down. GOD looks at the ledger and closes it. There is another moment of silence.*

More reprehensible however... the thousands of people who laughed and cheered you on as you made fun of him. Your followers.

TRUMP

I do not have thousands of followers. I have millions.

GOD

And they should have snuffed you out like a candle in the wind. But they didn't. Instead, they applauded you and boosted you up as you ridiculed him which somehow made them feel big and powerful. Shame on them. And then came the final blow when it was unthinkable you could go any lower, you did. You attacked the very people who died for

GOD (CONT'D)

your freedom to speak, and you chose to disparage them.

TRUMP

Like who?

GOD

Fallen service members who gave their lives for this country -- the country you and your followers claim to love yet are hell bent on destroying. And then to make matters worse, further disparaged the brave soldiers who died and called them "losers" and "suckers." We watched as you spat on the name of Gold Star soldier Humayun Khan and then attacked his parents and his mother Ghazala for remaining silent as she stood by her husband with dignity while grieving the death of her son. And if that weren't bad enough, you had the audacity to attack John McCain, a war hero who spent five years in a prison being tortured mercilessly when he was captured by the Viet Cong and you said:

GOD turns on the radio:

TRUMP'S VOICE (OVER RADIO)

"He wasn't a war hero. I like people who weren't captured."

TRUMP reacts to the sound of his voice and what he said.

TRUMP

Okay, well maybe I got caught up in the heat of the moment, but my followers still stood by me.

GOD

Astonishingly, they did. And it was at that moment in time when the universe saw the shift and needed to step in -- I needed to step in as I knew what we were dealing with. You're going to find out what it feels

GOD (CONT'D)

like to be captured and how well you'll hold up under those same circumstances. And we'll see if your followers will still stand by you.

TRUMP

They will.

> *The JANITOR comes down the ladder. He puts tools into his toolbox. He takes the ladder, opens the door marked #215 and exits.*

GOD

That said, we've been here before and seen the likes of you over the course of history.

TRUMP

There has never been anyone like me. Don't compare.

GOD

Bullies rear their ugly heads every so often -- some more famous than others. Whether they killed ten people or tens of millions, they're all the same. Rabid cult leaders like Manson or Mussolini, and of course, your idol: Hitler. Do you know what they all have in common?

TRUMP

I'm sure you're going to tell me.

> *THE JANITOR RE-ENTERS without the ladder. Dressed now in street clothes, he is folding his one-piece coverall and is now wearing a TRUMP T-SHIRT and a pair of jeans.*

GOD

They were all cowards. Like you. They never had the guts to personally kill anyone. Not one. They had their followers do their dirty work. Just like yours. You were given numerous chances to do the right thing on

GOD (CONT'D)

that infamous day in January when you unleashed a mob of violent bullies among civilized people. And you sat by watching as they erected gallows to hang Mike Pence and you did absolutely nothing. Senators and members of Congress ran for their lives terrorized; you did nothing. And for what? To overturn an election you know you lost? But it got worse. Your mob killed that day -- in your name and in mine.

TRUMP

They are God-fearing people.

GOD

They are not my people! They are yours. No one should fear me. Evoking my name when it suits you to create a world full of hate was the beginning of the end. Their end... and yet, days later, we watched those very same people turn around and beg for forgiveness because they were more afraid of your tweet than being chased down by a delusional mob of criminals with flag poles and guns which, to them was worse than being in your line of fire. Elected officials -- who knew better, who *knew* the truth -- abandoned any shred of moral compass they had left and chose someone who "grabs women by the pussy" as their leader. AND WHY?

Because they didn't want to lose their standing? Their imagined power... which they ended up giving away -- to you. But they lost far more... They lost their dignity and now stand at your feet devoted to a false idol. The irony is lost on no one except for them.

Which brings us full circle. You.

Deep down you know the truth, you know you lost, and you can't fathom losing. But the saddest irony of all is your followers believe in you more than you believe in yourself.

GOD (CONT'D)

When all is said and done, in the grand scheme of things, as you enter the realm of the universe, ultimately you will be seen as insignificant, nothing more than a bump on a pickle. A tiny spec that will fade away and you will go down in history as a man of many convictions without having any.

TRUMP stares at her. Then, he applauds: the claps are slow and deliberate.

TRUMP

Nice speech. And all without a teleprompter. Well done. *(He laughs)* You think you can make me "change my ways?" "See the light?!" Well, if I'm so "flawed," if you don't like who I am -- then change me. You fix it. THAT'S YOUR FUCKING JOB! What is it that people say? We're made in your image? If that's so, then how 'bout you fix yourself?! You want to talk about truth? The truth is people think you can help them and that's the biggest lie of all. You're the fraud. I am made in no one's image. I've made my own.

GOD tears the long calculator tape and folds it into a manageable size and hands it to TRUMP.

GOD

With that, you are being remanded to the custody of the universe where you will serve just over three million, one hundred and ninety-seven lifetimes.

She points to the shoes left by FRANKLIN, RUDY, ANNE, and IVANA.

Each person leaves a footprint. You will stand in each of their shoes: immigrants, captured veterans, Holocaust victims, abused women, and disabled members of society. Each step you take may bring you one step

GOD (CONT'D)

closer to understanding what it takes to be a human being and then you may move forward.

TRUMP

You will be hearing from my people.

GOD

I'm sure they will be quite vocal as they each set out on their personal journeys and relive the lives of those they harmed.

TRUMP

They will always stand by me.

TRUMP looks at the JANITOR who continues to listen.

GOD

Maybe. And we'll see how far they get as they walk in the shoes of those they harmed. Sadly, we have had to open a few new galaxies to accommodate the influx of new admissions. But you do have one final option to move forward and undo your sentence. And theirs.

TRUMP

Yeah? What?

GOD

Set the record straight.

TRUMP

How so?

GOD

Admit you lost.

TRUMP

Hell no.

GOD

Tell your followers the truth, fix the damage you created, change *their* fate.

TRUMP

And?

GOD

You will not have to relive every single day of those you harmed. One truth or three million, one hundred and ninety-seven lives relived.

TRUMP considers.

TRUMP

You're going to save me?

GOD

No. You are going to save yourself.

After a long beat.

TRUMP

That's your best offer: "the truth will set me free?" Why?

GOD

Because no one is their worst moment. Especially the ones you duped. The truth will set your followers free. You said they're willing to do anything for you, even die for you. Are you willing to save them from their fate?

GOD stands and opens the desk drawer. She tosses him an apple which he catches.

GOD opens the door marked "PRIVATE." The JANITOR stares at TRUMP.

Where do you stand?

THE SPOT RISES ON THE PAIRS OF SHOES.

GOD EXITS.

TRUMP tosses the apple up and down as he considers...

TRUMP
Person. Woman. Man. Camera. TV. Person. Woman. Man. God. Damn.

TRUMP STARES AT THE JANITOR as the LIGHTS FADE into darkness; a galaxy of stars illuminates the entire space.

The SPOT on the JANITOR and TRUMP slowly fades and the pairs of shoes remain illuminated until --

BLACKOUT

www.ingramcontent.com/pod-product-compliance
Lightning Source LLC
Chambersburg PA
CBHW071534120626
46550CB00006B/2452